Read About
Alex Rodriguez

David P. Torsiello

Enslow Elementary
an imprint of
Enslow Publishers, Inc.

40 Industrial Road
Box 398
Berkeley Heights, NJ 07922
USA

http://www.enslow.com

For Uncle Tony & all of the other Yankee fans in the family.

Enslow Elementary, an imprint of Enslow Publishers, Inc.

Enslow Elementary® is a registered trademark of Enslow Publishers, Inc.

Copyright © 2012 by Enslow Publishers, Inc.

Library of Congress Cataloging-in-Publication Data

Torsiello, David P.

  Read about Alex Rodriguez / David P. Torsiello.

    p. cm. — (I like sports stars!)

  Includes bibliographical references and index.

  Summary: "Alex Rodriguez is the third baseman for the New York Yankees. He is also known as one of the best home run hitters in the game"—Provided by publisher.

  ISBN 978-0-7660-3828-8

  1. Rodriguez, Alex, 1975- —Juvenile literature. 2. Baseball players—United States—Biography—Juvenile literature. I. Title.

  GV865.R62T67 2011

  796.357092—dc22

  [B]

                    2010029254

Paperback ISBN: 978-1-59845-302-7

Printed in the United States of America

062011 Lake Book Manufacturing, Inc., Melrose Park, IL

10 9 8 7 6 5 4 3 2 1

To Our Readers: We have done our best to make sure all Internet Addresses in this book were active and appropriate when we went to press. However, the author and the publisher have no control over and assume no liability for the material available on those Internet sites or on links to other Web sites. Any comments or suggestions can be sent by e-mail to comments@enslow.com or to the address on the back cover.

Every effort has been made to locate all copyright holders of material used in this book. If any errors or omissions have occurred, corrections will be made in future editions of this book.

Photo Credits: AP Images/Bill Kostroun, pp. 4, 23; AP Images/Carlos Osorio, pp. 8-9; AP Images/Charles Krupa, pp. 14-15; AP Images/Ed Betz, p. 6; AP Images/Ed Zurga, p. 10; AP Images/Elise Amendola, p. 22; AP Images/Frank Franklin II, pp. 1, 11; AP Images/Kathy Willens, p. 21; AP Images/Mark Duncan, p. 15 (inset); AP Images/Mary Altaffer, pp. 5, 13; AP Images/Tony Dejak, p. 7.

Cover Photo: AP Images/Frank Franklin II

Contents

Words to Know

baseball—A game that involves hitting a ball with a bat and running around bases.

home run—When a hitter hits the ball over the wall. The hitter and any runners on base ahead of him score.

playoffs—A series of games between several different teams that lead to the World Series.

third base—The base on the far left side of the field.

World Series—A series where two teams play to be champions of baseball. The winner must win four games out of seven.

Alex Rodriguez was born on July 27, 1975. He was born in New York City, not far from Yankee Stadium. Today, he plays third base for the Yankees!

Third base can be hard to play. You have to make throws across the field. You also have to catch the ball.

Alex is a good third baseman. Sometimes a runner will try to make it to third base. Alex has to tag him out!

Alex really loves to hit.
He is very good at
hitting home runs.

Alex may set new home run records. So, people like to get him to sign their baseballs. Alex tries to sign as many as he can.

After Alex hits the ball he has to run the bases. He is a good runner. Sometimes he will even steal a base!

Alex slides home under the catcher's tag. Safe! Alex just scored a run!

In the 2009 playoffs, Alex had a lot of big hits for the Yankees. In 15 games he hit 6 home runs!

19

Alex celebrates after hitting a home run to win another game!

After winning the World Series in 2009, Alex hugged his teammates. All of the Yankees got special rings for winning the Series. Alex wears his ring with pride!

Further Reading

Hoffman, Mary Ann. *Alex Rodriguez: Baseball Star*. New York: PowerKids Press, 2007.

Zuehlke, Jeffrey. *Alex Rodriguez*. Minneapolis: Lerner Publications, 2009.

Internet Address

The Official Site of Alex Rodriguez

http://www.arod.com/

INDEX

24